SUPER NIFTY
ORIGAMI
CRAFTS

Written by Andrea Urton
and Charlene Olexiewicz

Illustrated by Dianne O'Quinn Burke
Photographs by Ann Bogart

Lowell House
Juvenile
Los Angeles

CONTEMPORARY BOOKS

Chicago

NOTE: The numbered stars above the heading of each craft indicate the level of difficulty; one star being the easiest, three stars being the hardest.

Publisher: Jack Artenstein
General Manager, Juvenile Division: Elizabeth Amos
Director of Publishing Services: Rena Copperman
Editor in Chief, Juvenile Division, Nonfiction: Amy Downing
Managing Editor, Juvenile Division: Lindsey Hay
Art Director: Lisa-Theresa Lenthall
Crafts Artist: Charlene Olexiewicz
Model, page 13: Shannon Olexiewicz

Lowell House books can be purchased at special discounts when ordered in bulk for premiums and speical sales. Contact Department JH at the following address:

Lowell House Juvenile
2029 Century Park East, Suite 3290
Los Angeles, CA 90067

Library of Congress Catalog Card Number: 96-17221
· ISBN: 1-56565-396-3
10 9 8 7 6 5 4 3 2 1

CONTENTS

BEFORE YOU START

Now you can add spark to ordinary paper by turning it into origami art. Origami is an ancient oriental art that requires only a piece of paper, a little patience, and lots of creativity. Once you create your origami form, you can turn it into something really special by adding cotton, paint, glitter, ribbons, even googly eyes! So start folding, and get ready for great fun!

WHAT YOU'LL NEED

For folding your forms, any thin, square paper will do. You can buy origami craft paper that is colored on one side and white on the other at art supply and specialty stores. It's also precut into squares, with a standard size being about 6 inches. You may want to cut your own squares from gift-wrapping paper, thin wallpaper samples, colored photocopying paper, or notebook paper. Paper bags and construction paper work well for big designs, but for most projects they're too thick to make the nice, sharp folds you need.

In the art of origami, neatness does count. Always work on a smooth, hard surface, and make each crease as straight and crisp as possible. If you make a mistake, just chalk it up to experience and start over with a new piece of paper.

BASIC FOLDS

Step-by-step instructions are included for each project in this book. There are three basic folds you will use throughout:

VALLEY FOLD
Fold the paper toward you.

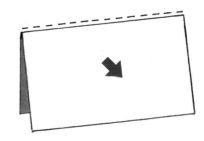

MOUNTAIN FOLD

Fold the paper away from you.

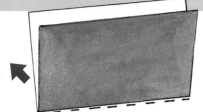

SQUASH FOLD

This fold is usually called for when two sides of a flap need to be squashed flat. To accomplish this, poke your finger inside the flap and—you guessed it—squash it.

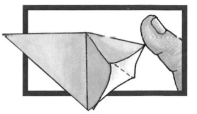

BASIC FORMS

Many origami crafts begin with one of several basic forms. Here you'll learn the forms that are the foundation for some of the origami projects in this book.

BASIC FORM 1

1 Begin with a piece of origami paper in a flat diamond shape, color side facedown. Fold your paper in half, bringing the top point to meet the bottom.

2 Now fold the far left and right points down to the center so that the points meet at the bottom of your form.

BASIC FORM 2

1 Begin with a square piece of paper in a flat diamond shape, color side facedown. Fold your paper in half, bringing the left point to meet the right point. Unfold to make a crease.

2 Fold the lower left and right sides to the center crease, so that your paper looks like a kite.

3 Then fold the upper left and right sides at the wide end of the kite to the center line and make two sharp creases. Now fold the form in half, bringing the bottom point to meet the top point.

4 Carefully open the form back to a kite. Then, while holding down point **A** with your fingertip, lift up point **B** and bring it down to point **C**. Repeat the same fold with point **D**.

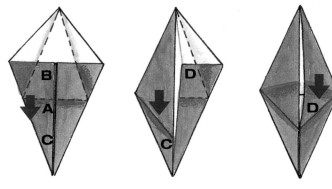

BASIC FORM 3

1 Fold your square piece of paper in half from side to side. Next, open the paper, then fold it from top to bottom. Reopen the paper and fold it diagonally both ways. Now when you reopen the paper to a square you should have the pattern of creases as shown.

2 Fold the top half of the paper to meet the bottom half to make a rectangle. Then fold the left side to meet the right side so that you have a square. The square should have the open ends facing down and to the right.

3 Now hold the top flap up straight and poke your finger inside until it reaches the very tip. Squash the flap down to form a triangle. Be sure all your corners line up and look pointed. Now turn the form over and repeat this step on the other side.

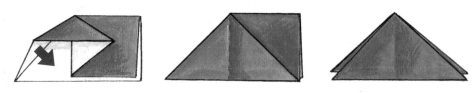

HOT-AIR BALLOON

WHAT YOU'LL NEED

- origami paper
- scissors
- small piece of cardboard
- glue
- wire cutters
- pipe cleaners
- tape
- variety of stickers

DIRECTIONS

 1 To make the balloon part of this piece, begin with **BASIC FORM 3** and fold the bottom left and right points (front flaps only) to the top center point; then turn the form over and repeat this step.

2 Now fold the left and right points to the center, turn the form over again, and repeat this step on the other side. Folding and unfolding softens the paper and makes it more pliable.

3 Fold and unfold points **A** and **B** (front flaps only) to make a sharp crease. Next, tuck points **A** and **B** into the center triangles as shown, then turn your form over and repeat this step on the other side. Finally, turn the flap, blow into the hole at the bottom of the form, and your balloon will inflate before your eyes.

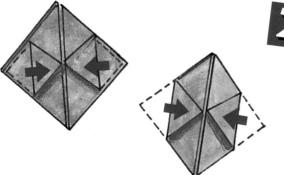

4 To make the basket, begin with **BASIC FORM 3**, open end facing away from you, then fold over point **A** (front flap only). Now fold point **A** back and tuck the tip inside the top of the form.

5 Repeat step 4 with the other side of the form, then turn the form over and repeat step 4 with both sides. Your form should look like the one shown here.

6 Fold point **B** up and back to make a sharp crease. Gently slip your finger inside and open the basket while flattening the base at point **B**.

7 Strengthen the bottom of the basket by cutting a square out of cardboard slightly smaller than the base. Put a dab of glue on the square and slip it into the origami basket, glue side down.

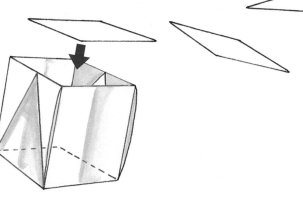

8 Using the wire cutters, cut four equal lengths of pipe cleaner. About ¼ inch down, bend one end of each pipe cleaner into a right angle. Glue the four pipe cleaners into the basket, one in each corner. Be sure that the bent ends touch the bottom of the basket and point to the center. To help them stay in place while drying, you may need to tape the pipe cleaners to the inside of the basket.

About ¼ inch down from the ends, bend the tops of all four pipe cleaners toward the center. This will create a perch for the balloon to rest on. Put a dab of glue on top of each pipe cleaner and place the balloon on top. Allow the glue to dry. Finally, decorate the balloon and basket with a variety of stickers.

SUPER NIFTY IDEA!

Prove that your balloon is full of something more than just hot air. Fill the basket with jelly beans, gum balls, and candies, and use it as a nifty candy dish!

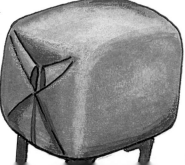

You'll soon be up, up, and away, floating high above the clouds in your new hot-air balloon made of paper and fueled by your imagination!

THIS LITTLE PIGGY

WHAT YOU'LL NEED

- origami paper
- glue
- two googly eyes
- curling ribbon

- scissors
- pink felt
- black marking pen

DIRECTIONS

1 Begin with a square and fold the top edge to meet the bottom edge. Unfold, and now fold the top and bottom edges to meet the center crease. Then turn the form over and fold the left edge to the right edge. Unfold and fold the left and right sides to meet at the center crease.

2 Next, pull out point **A** on the upper left square as shown, and flatten it into a triangle. Now repeat this step with each of the squares.

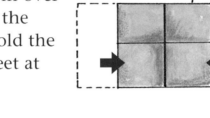

3 Using a **MOUNTAIN FOLD**, turn back points **B** and **C** to make a square. Now open up point **D** to lie flat. It won't be long now before your plump little porker takes shape. Use a **VALLEY FOLD** to fold the form in half, moving the bottom edge up to the top edge. Secure the sides together with glue.

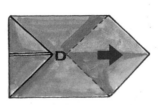
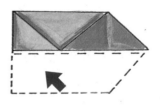

4 You're ready to make the legs by pulling out point **E** (front flap only) and point **F** (front flap only) as shown. Repeat on the other side of the form.

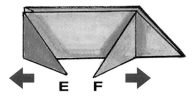

 5 With your finger, push in point **G** until you've created a flat snout as shown here.

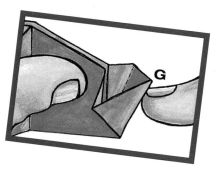

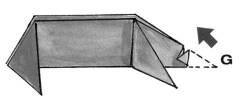

6 Glue on two googly eyes. Curl a 3-inch length of ribbon and glue it on for a tail. If the tail is too long, trim any excess.

7 For ears, cut two small triangles from pink felt and glue onto the piggy. For the snout, cut a circle from pink felt. Use the black marker to make two black dots for nostrils. Glue onto snout to complete your piggy.

SUPER NIFTY IDEA!

How about making an entire pig family? Use medium- and large-size origami paper to make a ma and pa. With smaller pieces, you can create little piglets!

Here are a few fine, plump pigs playing in the mud! Don't forget to give your pig a curly tail to wiggle, too.

HATFUL OF FUN

WHAT YOU'LL NEED

- origami or wrapping paper
- wire cutters
- wire garland (available at craft or party stores)
- stapler
- scissors
- assorted colors of curling ribbon
- hole punch
- large round marker
- elastic cord

DIRECTIONS

1 For a hat to fit your head, you'll need a piece of paper minimum size 18 inches by 18 inches. Begin with **BASIC FORM 1**, with the two loose points facing you. Only fold up the front flaps of the two bottom points to the top point. Then fold these two points out to the sides as shown.

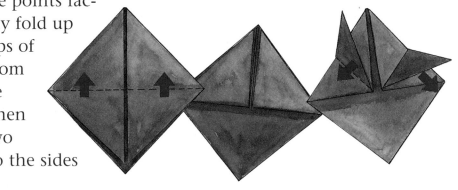

2 Take the new front bottom flap and fold up three-quarters of it toward the top of the hat. Then take the bottom edge of this flap and fold it up to the halfway point. Next, tuck in the back flap, and your hat is ready to be decorated.

3 With wire cutters, cut a length of wire garland for the rim of the hat. Secure garland onto hat with three or four staples.

4 Cut 24-inch lengths of curling ribbon. With the hole punch, punch a hole through the hat, ½ inch down from the top point. Gather the ribbon ends together and thread them through the hole. When the ribbons are pulled halfway through, secure them to the hat by tying them in a knot. Have an adult help you use the scissors to curl the ribbons.

5 Cut a 10-inch length of garland. Twist it into a spiral by winding it around a large-size marker. Straighten out about ¾ inch of one end of the spiral and insert it through the hole at the top front of the hat. Twist this small piece of wire around the spiraled garland until it is secure.

6 Make a chin strap for your hat using the elastic cord. Hold one end of the elastic at the top of one of your ears, and go under your chin to the top of your other ear. Without stretching the elastic, cut the length that you measured. Tie a double knot at each end. Staple the elastic onto the hat just below the knots. Now you (and your hat) are ready to party!

By using paper of different sizes, you can make a hat to fit anyone. You can even use gift-wrapping paper to make an extra special headpiece.

SUPER NIFTY IDEA!
● ● ● ● ● ● ● ● ● ●
Make a festive hat for each one of your friends next time you throw a party. Pick a wrapping-paper print that goes with the party theme. Glue on confetti, glitter, colorful buttons, beads, or hard candies.

CREATIVE CANDLE CRADLE

WHAT YOU'LL NEED

- foil-backed origami paper
- candle (8 inches or shorter)
- strong craft glue
- assorted color rhinestones
- assorted color sequins (regular, round, or any other shape)

DIRECTIONS

1 Begin with a square piece of paper. Fold the paper in half from side to side, then top to bottom to form the creases shown. Then reopen it into a square.

2 Fold the upper left and lower right corners into the center. Then fold the upper right and the lower left corners into the center. Turn the form over, and fold the four corners into the center. Carefully fold the four points back to meet the outside edges of the form. So far so good?

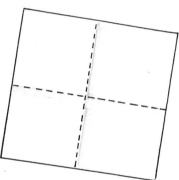

3 Using a **MOUNTAIN FOLD**, fold the form in half, then push the upper left and right corners toward the center and tuck them in as shown, forming a triangle.

Be sure your form is nice and flat, then fold and unfold the top small triangle to make a sharp crease.

 Loosely open the form and push the middle of the "star" down and in to form a four-pointed indentation in the center. Finally, you may want to unfold the four original points, creating more of a bowl in which to set the candle.

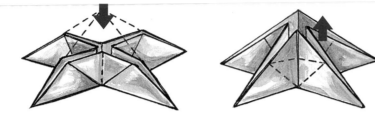

 Decorate your star-shaped candleholder by gluing on rhinestones and sequins in an assortment of colors. Be sure to use a strong, extra-tacky craft glue, since regular glue will not stick to a foil surface. You can use star-shaped sequins as shown here, or any other shape of your choice.

7 Insert an 8-inch candle. (Light the candle only with the help of an adult.) Enjoy!

SUPER NIFTY IDEA!
• • • • • • • • • • •

Somebody special having a birthday? Put one of these super nifty candle cradles right-dab in the middle of the birthday cake. Then tell the special birthday boy or girl to make one terrific wish and blow!

Can a piece of paper be strong enough to support a candle? It can if you fold it the origami way! For a festive candleholder, make this form with metallic foil-backed origami paper.

A WHALE OF AN IDEA

WHAT YOU'LL NEED

- 18-by-18-inch piece of wrapping paper
- tape
- glue
- two (¾-inch) googly eyes
- 18-inch length of bendable wire
- four or five cotton balls
- wire cutters

DIRECTIONS

1 Take an 18-by-18-inch square of wrapping paper. Begin with **BASIC FORM 2**. Turn the form over so that the two loose flaps in the center are facedown, pointing toward of your left hand. Fold the top and bottom points to the center crease and the left side toward the middle.

2 Fold the top side in a **VALLEY FOLD** to meet the bottom side, then fold back the whale's fins on both sides.

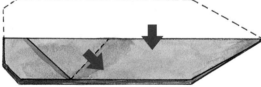

3 Now make the creases as shown near point **D**. While holding the tail just below the first crease, spread the tip open and up.

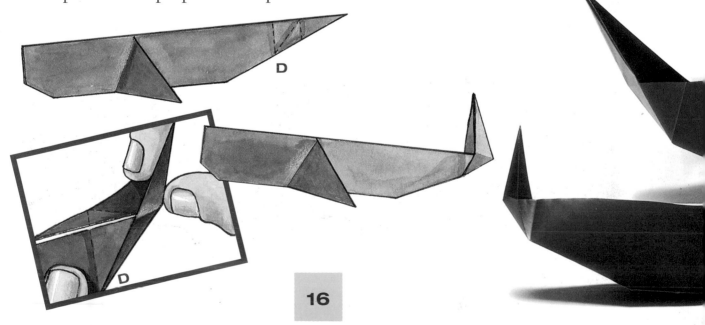

4 To help your whale stay upright, tape the bottom flaps together. Glue on googly eyes.

5 To make a spout, bend the wire in half. Now, shred the cotton balls together into one big ball. Insert the doubled-up wire, ends first, into the center of the cotton. Push it through, stopping when the top of the wire first disappears into the cotton. To make a spout stem, pull some cotton from the base of the ball and twist it around the wire, going down about 1 inch.

6 To complete the stand for the spout, spread the two wires apart, just under the stem, into a V. Bend the wire at a right angle as shown. This creates the base. If the base is longer than 1½ inches, cut the excess with wire cutters.

7 Open up the seam at the top of the whale and insert the V-shaped spout stand as shown. You may need to adjust the width of the V to match up with the whale. Once in place, put a dab of glue at the V to secure the spout stand to the whale.

By using a large square of gift-wrapping paper, you can make a really big whale. Add a spout and yell, "Thar she blows!"

SUPER NIFTY IDEA!
· · · · · · · · · · ·

Doing a science-fair project or report at school that relates to the ocean or sea life? Liven up your display by adding this whale to create an A+ tidal wave!

THE STAR ATTRACTION

WHAT YOU'LL NEED

- **colored origami paper**
- **needle and thread**
- **rhinestones, beads, etc.**

- **scissors**
- **glue**

DIRECTIONS

1 Fold your square piece of paper in half from side to side. Next, open the paper to a square, then fold it from top to bottom. Reopen the paper and fold it diagonally both ways, then unfold. It should be in a diamond shape in front of you, color side facedown. Now fold the paper in half, bringing the top point down to meet the bottom point.

2 Hold the right side of the form open at point **A**, then **SQUASH-FOLD** it by pushing down on it to meet point **B**. Repeat this step with the form's left side.

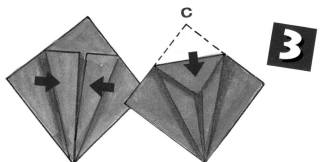

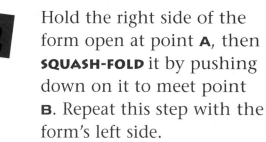

3 Using only the top layer of paper, fold the lower left and right sides to the center line, then fold down point **C**. Unfold the form back to a small diamond, as in step 2.

4 Lift up point **D** (top layer only), fold it back at the crease, then flatten it into a long diamond shape.

5 Turn the form over and repeat steps 3 and 4. With the two open points up, fold point **E** (front flap only) up to meet points **F** and **G**. Then turn the form over and fold and unfold points **F** and **G** to make creases as shown.

6 Now lift the left triangle until it is perpendicular to the form. Slip your finger into the opening on the back side of the raised triangle. Open it slightly.

7 On the center of the star, push down and out to flatten the left triangle. Repeat this step on the right side of the form.

8 To attach a string to your star, put a 10-inch length of thread into a needle. Push the needle through the top point of the star. Remove the needle from the thread, then tie the two ends of the threads into a knot. Finally, glue sequins and beads to decorate your star.

SUPER NIFTY IDEA!

Try a red and green color scheme on your star for Christmas or blue and white for Hanukkah. Use glitter paint to add that holiday sparkle!

This four-pointed star is fun to make and is a perfect decoration for holiday packages.

FLUTTERING BUTTERFLY

WHAT YOU'LL NEED

- origami paper
- pipe cleaners
- wire cutters
- glue
- scissors

DIRECTIONS

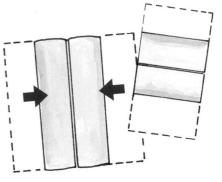

1 Begin with your paper folded with the first step in **BASIC FORM 3**, then unfold it so it is lying flat in a square shape. Fold the right and left sides so that they meet the center line. Now fold the bottom and top edges so that they meet the center line; then make a nice sharp crease and unfold the top and bottom edges only.

2 Make two diagonal creases across the center four squares only. Do this first by folding point **A** to meet point **B**. Crease the paper sharply, then unfold it. Now repeat this step on the opposite side, bringing point **C** to meet point **D**.

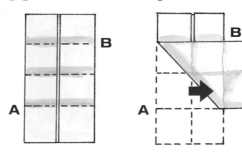

3 This next step is tricky, so look closely at the illustration for help. First, grasp the bottom two corners. Then lift them up and gently tug them apart so that they flatten and the bottom edge meets the center. Repeat this step with the top two corners, only this time pull them down to meet the center.

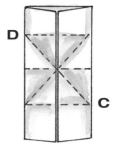

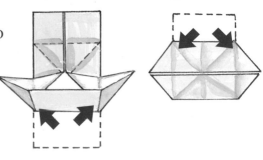

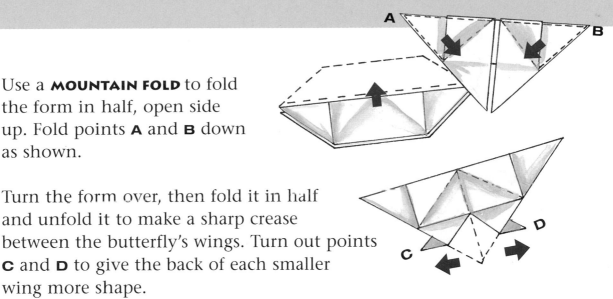

4 Use a **MOUNTAIN FOLD** to fold the form in half, open side up. Fold points **A** and **B** down as shown.

5 Turn the form over, then fold it in half and unfold it to make a sharp crease between the butterfly's wings. Turn out points **C** and **D** to give the back of each smaller wing more shape.

6 For the body, bend a pipe cleaner in half. Twist it once around at the spot that is to be the head. Spread out the two pipe cleaner ends to create antennae. Cut any excess with the wire cutters and glue body onto wings.

SUPER NIFTY IDEA!

Make a mobile full of fluttering butterflies! Make six to eight butterflies, varying their sizes, colors, and designs. Using thread, tie them onto a stick or a wire hanger.

7 Add beautiful designs to your butterfly by cutting out colorful shapes from orgami paper. Shapes can include triangles, teardrops, stripes, and so on. Glue the shapes onto the butterfly's wings.

Use several sheets of different colored paper to make a bevy of beautiful butterflies.

ROCK-A-BYE PAPOOSE

WHAT YOU'LL NEED

- origami paper
- colored pencils, brown and pink
- fine-tipped black marker
- black yarn
- glue
- assorted tiny glass beads
- thread
- tape
- scissors

DIRECTIONS

1 Begin with a square piece of paper in a flat diamond shape. Bring the right point to meet the left point and crease. Unfold. Now fold the lower left and right sides to the center crease, so that your paper looks like a kite. Use a **MOUNTAIN FOLD** to fold back the top triangle. Next, fold the top left and right sides in to the center crease and turn your form over.

2 This part is a little tricky, so go slowly. Lift the upper square (the papoose's head), reach inside, and fold points **A** and **B** to the center.

3 To complete your papoose form, fold back the top and bottom points on the head, and the bottommost point of the form.

4 Using the brown pencil, lightly color in the face. Use the pink pencil to add color to the cheeks. Put on the features (eyes, nose, and mouth) with the black marker. To get a "baby" look, be sure to draw the features low on the head, leaving the forehead large.

5 Cut a few strands of black yarn for hair. (Remember, babies do not have much hair!) Glue the hair on and allow to dry.

6 Make an Indian necklace for your papoose by stringing some tiny glass beads onto thread. Stop when your string of beads is long enough to go across the front of the baby under the chin. Put the necklace on the papoose and tie the thread with a knot at the back. To keep the necklace from shifting, put a piece of tape on the back, trapping the thread underneath. A spot of glue at center front will also keep the necklace in place.

7 Decorate the front of the form—the blanket— with cutout zigzags and strips of colorful origami paper. Glue these shapes onto the blanket.

8 Finally, cut out a headband and feather from origami paper and secure them onto the head with glue.

SUPER NIFTY IDEA!

Just glue a Popsicle® stick to the back of the little papoose and place it among the flowers to make a wonderful addition to the family's Thanksgiving centerpiece!

This little papoose comes wrapped in its own Indian blanket.

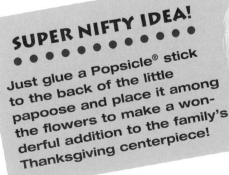

HOME, HAUNTED HOME

WHAT YOU'LL NEED

- origami paper
- scissors
- glue

- ribbon
- black fine-tip marker

DIRECTIONS

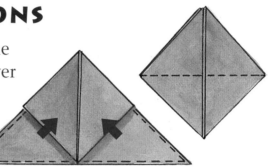

1 Begin with **BASIC FORM 3**, then fold the right and left bottom corners (top layer only) up to the center point. Turn the form over and repeat this step with the remaining layer. You now have a diamond shape.

2 Fold the bottom point up to the top point to make a crease and unfold; then lift up the triangle on the right side and move point **A** down to form a square. Lift up the triangle on the left side and move point **B** down to form a square. Then turn the form over and repeat this step on the other side.

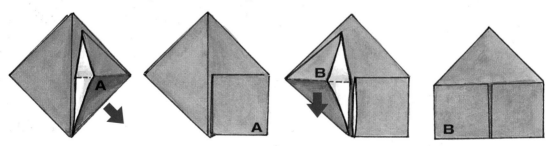

3 Fold outer sides 1 and 2 (top layer only) to the center to make a crease, then unfold again. Fold and unfold triangle shapes on each "door," making creases as shown.

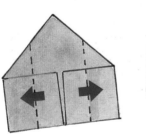

24

To create the large front door, use the creases that you made as guidelines and fold point **C** to meet point **A**, and point **D** to meet point **B**. To finish the form, fold up the center triangle.

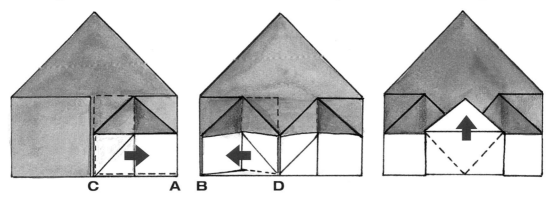

C A B D

Now you're ready to decorate! You can follow the picture below as a guide or create your own original house of horrors. Use ribbon, cotton pieces, and whatever else you can find to make this the creepiest haunt on the block!

SUPER NIFTY IDEA!

Create a completely frightful scene by taping your house onto the center inside of a shoe box lid. Fill the lid with sand. Use bare twigs for dead trees and place them throughout the graveyard. Now say, "BOO!"

With its creaky shutters and ghostly apparitions, this haunted house will make your knees knock in fright!

CHATTERING BIRD

WHAT YOU'LL NEED

- origami paper
- assorted colorful craft feathers
- strong craft glue
- scissors
- two googly eyes

DIRECTIONS

1 First, complete the instructions for **BASIC FORM 2**. Next, fold the bottom point to meet the top point. This will make a triangle with two smaller triangles inside. Gently grasp the tips of each of the smaller triangles and pull them out to the sides. Once you have a shape that looks something like a crown, fold and unfold the form, creasing it in half lengthwise.

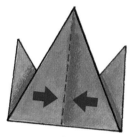

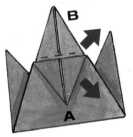

2 To give the bird a beak, simply fold point **A** toward you and point **B** away from you. Crease the paper sharply, then unfold point **B**.

3 Fold and unfold both halves of the beak to make the creases pictured in the illustration.

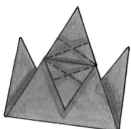

4 Finally, fold the wings away from you and behind the bird until they meet in the back. As you do this, the beak will start to close. Pull carefully on the ends of the beak until the form is flat. Make all folds sharp. Then reopen the form a little to make the bird three-dimensional.

5 Now your fine-feathered friend needs feathers! Use an assortment of colorful craft feathers and glue them onto the bird's head, chest, and wings. If the feathers are too long, simply use the scissors to trim them before you glue them on. Glue on the two googly eyes above the beak.

SUPER NIFTY IDEA!

Gather old plastic grass or shred up colorful wrapping paper into thin strips. Bundle up the strips to form a cozy little nest. Place your perky feathered friend into its new home!

With your help, this bird will flap its wings and open and close its beak. You can almost hear it chattering.

FRIENDSHIP RING

WHAT YOU'LL NEED

- origami paper (4½ inches square)
- scissors
- assorted charms and/or beads
- strong craft glue

DIRECTIONS

1 Cut a piece of origami paper into three equal pieces. You will be using one-third sheet for each ring you make.

2 Now fold one of the pieces of paper in half lengthwise, and unfold. Fold the outer edges into the center crease, then fold the paper in half to make a long, thin strip.

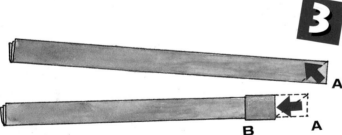

3 At one end of the strip, fold and unfold point **A**, then fold over the left edge at the straight crease to form a square, allowing point **A** to meet point **B**.

4 Fold over two more times, unfold to a long strip again, then use a **MOUNTAIN FOLD** to turn point **C** back to meet point **D** as shown.

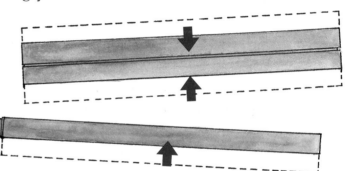

5 Use a **MOUNTAIN FOLD** to fold point **E** back to meet point **F**. You have now formed a thick triangle at the back of your ring, and your paper should look like an L on its side.

6 Now use a **VALLEY FOLD** to fold the upper leg of the L down. Tuck the lower square behind the form and into the triangle at the back of the ring.

7 Finally, fold back the two corners into a point at the other end of the strip, curl it around, and tuck it into the open end of the square. If your ring is too large, cut some length off the long end of the strip before you tuck it in. Now use the other two pieces of paper to make two more rings.

8 Select a charm or bead for each ring. Keeping the personalities of your friends in mind, select one that matches his or her personality. Glue the charm or bead onto the ring using strong craft glue. Allow to dry. Once your friends see these super nifty rings, they'll want to make some, too.

SUPER NIFTY IDEA!

As your collection of rings grows, how about stringing them onto a colorful plastic cord or length of yarn, making them into a friendship necklace.

With one piece of paper you can make a trio of rings—one for you and two more for friends.

ANGELIC ORIGAMI

WHAT YOU'LL NEED

- colored origami paper
- flesh-colored origami paper
- fine-line black marker
- pink marker, crayon, or pencil
- glue
- pipe cleaners
- tape
- wire cutters
- scissors
- ribbon
- doily
- glitter paint
- cotton balls or pillow stuffing

DIRECTIONS

1 Begin with **BASIC FORM 1**, with the opening in the back and the two loose triangles pointing down. Then fold the upper left and right sides to the center line. Next, unfold the back flaps. These will soon be the angel's wings.

2 Now fold point **A** over to the left and crease it well; then fold it back to the right as shown. You now have a little flap across the center line. This is point **B**. Use a **VALLEY FOLD** to fold it in the same direction as point **A**.

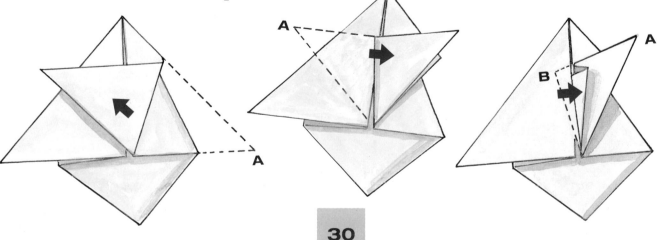

3 Repeat step 2 on the left side of the form, then turn the form over. To give your angel heavenly detail, fold in points **C** and **D**. Use a **MOUNTAIN FOLD** to turn back point **E**. This flap will allow your angel to stand.

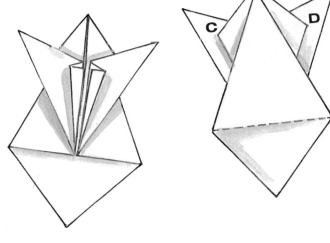

4 Now it's time to add the details. For the head, cut out two circles the same size from the flesh-colored origami paper. On one of the circles, draw a sweet face using the fine-line black marker. Color in cheeks using a pink marker, crayon, or pencil.

5 Attach the head by spreading glue onto the white sides of both circles. Take the angel body, front side up, and place it on top of the glued side of the blank circle. Make sure to overlap the body at least ½ inch as shown. Now carefully place the circle with the face on top of the body, making sure to align it with the other circle. The result is that the body is "sandwiched" between both circles.

6 Bend one end of a pipe cleaner into a circle for a halo. Place the remaining straight end down the back of the angel. Secure the pipe cleaner onto the angel using a few pieces of tape. Cut off excess pipe cleaner. With scissors, curl a few lengths of ribbon and glue on for hair. Or, glue on straight ribbon, as shown below.

7 For the final touches, cut a small piece of paper doily for a lace collar and glue it on under the chin. Add sparkle to the wings with glitter paint. Set your angel upon a fluffy cloud of cotton balls or pillow stuffing.

How can paper be angelic? You'll see when you fold this lovely origami angel that can stand in a window or on a mantel as a perfect holiday decoration.

SUPER NIFTY IDEA!

Create an angel tree by making several angels and hanging them on the tree as holiday ornaments. Tie a loop of thread onto the halo for hanging. At the very top of the tree, why not make a large golden halo with yellow pipe cleaners—now that's an angelic tree!